Forms of Energy

Revised Edition

Anna Claybourne

capstone

©2010, 2016 Raintree
an imprint of Capstone Global Library, LLC
Chicago, Illinois

To contact Capstone Global Library, please
call 800-747-4992, or visit our web site
www.mycapstone.com

Edited by James Nixon
Designed by Ian Winton
Original illustrations © Discovery Books 2009
Illustrated by Stefan Chabluk
Picture research by James Nixon
Originated by Modern Age

**Library of Congress Cataloging-in-Publication Data
is available on the Library of Congress website.**
ISBN 978-1-4109-8532-3 (paperback)
ISBN 978-1-4109-8382-4 (ebook)

Image Credits
Corbis: Larry Lee Photography, 20; iStockphoto: 8
Right, 26&27, eROMAZe, 28 Top, Fertnig, 12, Cover,
NRedmond, 6 (stove), Pavelk, 6 (lamp), Rsmith19, 29
Bottom; NASA: 22 Bottom; Science Source: Clouds Hill
Imaging Ltd, 15, Ted Kinsman, 17 Top; Shutterstock:
11 Top, 11 Middle, 13, 22 Top, 23 Right, A-R-T, 10
Bottom, Adam Gryko, 30 Top, Adrian Steele, 19 Top,
Alexandre17, 41 (stereo), Brian A Jackson, 3 Bottom,
Brian A Jackson, 39, 40 (power station), bubamarac,
41 (train), Casey K. Bishop, 17 Bottom, Catwalk Photos,
9 Bottom, Coppered, 32 (stereo), curraheeshutter,
36&37, cynoclub, 41 (fan), Denphumi, 41 (lightbulb),
djgis, 33 (sun), Dmitry Pistrov, 41 (street lights), emin
kuliyev, 4&5, Eugene Berman, 34, Fedorov Oleksiy,
24, Fer Gregory, 32 (tv), FooTToo, 32 (satellite), Galina
Barskaya, 6 (girl), Germanskydiver, 7 (skydiving),
ljansempoi, 41 (remote), Image Point Fr, 10 Top,
irabel8, 21, Ivanagott, 33 Top, Jamen Percy, 40 (oil),
Jayakumar, 33 (x-ray), JENNY SHULER, 25 (lizard),
JetKat, 41 (plane), Joe Gough, 38, Junne, 40 (dam),
Ken Schulze, 31, Lindasj22, 41 (house), Lori Skelton,
25 (hawk), Marafona, 28 Bottom, Marjan Veljanoski,
41 (iron), marlee, 40 (nuclear power), Mau Horng, 25
(cockroach), maxim ibragimov, 33 (tv), mikeledray,
29 Top, MilanMarkovic78, 28 Middle, Nadalina, 25
(earth), nadiya_sergey, 25 (sun), Natalia Mikhaylova,
9 Top, newphotoservice, 40&41 Bottom Right, Noel
Powell, 3 Top, 30 Bottom, NorGal, 40 (stove), nosonjai,
7 (spaghetti), pixelman, 40 (coal), pixpax, 40 (solar
energy), Racheal Grazias, 18, Roxana Gonzalez, 16,
schankz, 33 (sign), Shannon Matteson, 7 (chainsaw),
Stephen Coburn, 23 Left, Stephen Meese, 40 (wind
farm), Steve Pepple, 11 Bottom, STILLFX, 27, sunyaluk,
6 (pylon), Suzanne Tucker, 6 (cyclist), Triff, 1, Umberto
Shtanzman, 32 (phone), VICTOR TORRES, 41 (laptop),
Thinkstock: Comstock, Cover Top; Wikimedia: 8, Left

We would like to thank content consultant Suzy
Gazlay and text consultant Nancy Harris for their
invaluable help in the preparation of this book.

Contents

How fast does light go as it zooms through space? Find out on page 31!

Where does the electricity supply in your home come from? Find out on page 40!

Some words are shown in bold, **like this**. These words are explained in the glossary. You will find important information and definitions underlined, <u>**like this**</u>.

What Is ENERGY?

All the time, everywhere you look, things are happening. People run, walk, and talk; trains rattle along tracks; planets zoom through space; fires burn; thunderstorms rumble. All these things can only happen because of **energy**. Energy is what makes things move, happen, and change.

<u>Energy is the ability to do work.</u> This means that energy is used whenever anything happens. For example, if you kick a ball, pick up a pen, or carry a shopping bag home, you use energy. It also takes energy to light a lamp or to make a hairdryer or a computer work.

Energy can exist even when nothing seems to be happening. For example, energy can be stored in a **battery**, in food, or in **fuel**, such as coal.

Raisin power
Eating a large handful of raisins gives you energy to run farther and faster!

WHAT IS "WORK"?

When you hear the word "work," you might think of people doing jobs or schoolwork, or hard work like digging a hole. But when we are talking about energy, "work" means any kind of activity or movement that makes something happen. So, for example, making a lightbulb glow is a kind of "work" that energy can do.

It takes a lot of energy to light up all the signs and buildings in this busy city and to make the cars and buses move around.

FORMS OF ENERGY

There are several different types, or forms, of **energy**. They work in different ways and make different kinds of things happen. Energy can be **kinetic energy** (moving energy) or **potential energy** (energy that is stored, ready to use).

Here are some of the main forms of energy you will find in everyday life:

FORMS OF KINETIC ENERGY

KINETIC ENERGY This is the name for the energy of moving objects, such as a bike.

ELECTRICAL ENERGY This is a form of kinetic energy that can collect in an object or flow along a wire. It powers many of our machines and gadgets.

HEAT ENERGY (also called **thermal** energy). Heat energy makes objects feel hot, and heat up other objects. It happens because of the movement of **molecules**, the tiny units that **matter** (or stuff) is made of.

LIGHT ENERGY Light is a kind of kinetic energy that can move across space. It glows from the Sun, fire, and electric lights.

SOUND ENERGY When you hear a sound, such as a guitar playing, it is because a form of energy makes the air **vibrate**, or shake back and forth. This movement means that sound is a kind of kinetic energy.

FORMS OF POTENTIAL ENERGY

Energy spotting

Make a chart listing all the forms of energy, and try to match each one to things that happen around you in everyday life.

Sound energy → Radio on at breakfast time.

Light energy → Bedside lamp. Sunshine.

Kinetic energy → Throwing a stick for the dog.

Chemical energy → Breakfast. Snacks.

GRAVITATIONAL POTENTIAL ENERGY is potential energy due to gravity. When a plane carries a skydiver into the sky, he gathers a store of potential energy. When he jumps out, the potential energy turns into kinetic energy as he falls.

CHEMICAL ENERGY
Chemical energy is a kind of potential energy stored in substances, such as **fuel** and food.

ELASTIC POTENTIAL ENERGY is potential energy stored in a spring or elastic substance. If you stretch an elastic band, it holds a store of elastic potential energy. When you let go, this is released as kinetic energy as the band flies back to its normal shape.

NUCLEAR ENERGY
This is a form of potential energy stored in **atoms**.

Electrical energy powers this chainsaw and makes it work. As the chainsaw works, it makes movement and sound energy.

Changing form

Not only are there different forms of energy, but energy can also change from one form to another. This is called **energy conversion** or **energy transformation**.

For example, if you burn a pile of wood, the chemical energy it contains changes to heat and light energy. When you switch on an electric food mixer, a flow of **electricity** changes into kinetic energy (movement) as the blades whizz around.

Conservation of energy

When energy is used, it does not get "used up." It just keeps changing form. This is called the **Law of Conservation of Energy** (conservation means "keeping"). <u>**Energy cannot be created or destroyed.**</u> <u>**It can only change from one form to another**</u>.

James Joule 1818–1889

English scientist James Prescott Joule studied heat, electricity, and other forms of energy.

paddle

water

barrel

He found that when water moved, it warmed up slightly. He made a paddle swish around in a barrel of water and carefully measured how much warmer the water became. A certain amount of work resulted in the same rise in temperature. The energy used in working the paddle was simply transformed into heat energy. This experiment helped to reveal the Law of Conservation of Energy. Joule also gave his name to the **joule**, a unit of measurement for energy.

Energy transfer

Energy transfer means moving energy from one place to another. This can happen when energy changes form—such as when a flow of electricity in a wire changes into movement in a machine. However, it can also happen when energy does not change form. For example, if you throw a ball, the energy transfers from your moving arm to the moving ball. It has transferred to a different place, but it has not changed form.

When a horse eats, it takes in chemical energy from its food. In its body, the chemical energy is converted (changed) into other forms of energy, such as movement. A horse needs plenty of food to get the energy for a show-jumping competition.

Escaping energy

When energy is used to do work, some of it escapes, or **dissipates**. It doesn't disappear, as energy cannot be destroyed. Instead, it usually changes into heat energy and escapes into the air. **The way energy escapes as it changes form is called dissipation.**

TRY THIS

FEEL HEAT ESCAPING

Look for machines in your home that are not designed to make heat. When they are being used, carefully put your hand near them to see if heat is escaping from them.

You could try:
- A laptop computer
- A cell phone
- A game console
- A radio

14:25

A thermograph is a type of image that shows heat. In this thermograph of a girl using a computer, the red and yellow areas show where a lot of heat is escaping.

10

Energy efficiency

A lightbulb is designed to turn electricity into light energy. But some of the electricity changes into heat instead of light. The lightbulb gets hot, and heat escapes into the air.

If a machine or system does not lose very much energy when it works, it is said to be **efficient** or **energy-efficient**.

Old-fashioned lightbulbs are not very energy-efficient. About 10 percent of the electricity they use turns into light, while 90 percent turns into heat!

Modern energy-saving lightbulbs are more efficient. Only about 50 percent of the electricity turns into heat.

old-fashioned lightbulb

energy-saving lightbulb

Oil in the machine

Heat often escapes when moving parts of machines rub together. This rubbing is called **friction**. <u>**Friction between two surfaces turns kinetic energy into heat energy.**</u> We can reduce friction, and make machines more efficient, by lubricating them (making them slippery) with oil.

Body heat

In cold weather, a lot of heat escapes from body parts, such as your face, head, and hands, if they are not covered up. Heat in your body comes from chemical energy in the food you eat.

Heat Energy

Heat energy, or thermal energy, is everywhere. It constantly spreads out from warmer objects to colder objects. Everything around us has some heat in it—even things that feel really cold.

Moving molecules

You know what heat feels like—you can sense it when you touch a warm radiator, or eat hot toast. But what is heat? In fact, it all has to do with **molecules**—the tiny units a substance is made of. The hotter a substance is, the more the molecules in it jiggle or zoom around.

In fact, because heat is caused by molecule movement, it is actually a type of **kinetic energy,** or movement energy. **Heat is a form of energy associated with movement of molecules in a substance.**

Welding equipment, used to join pieces of metal together by melting them, can reach incredibly high temperatures of around 20,000°C (36,000°F).

Heat and temperature

Heat is not quite the same thing as temperature. Heat is a form of energy that flows from one object to another. Temperature is a measurement of the heat energy level in a particular substance.

You can measure temperature using a **thermometer**, with a temperature scale, such as Celsius or Fahrenheit. As heat is a form of energy, it is measured in **joules**.

The two scales both measure temperature in degrees, but Fahrenheit degrees are closer together and the two scales do not match up.

Celsius scale

Fahrenheit scale

A thermometer has a glass tube containing a liquid that expands (gets bigger) as it warms up. The warmer the temperature, the higher the liquid pushes up the tube.

°C   °F

50	120
40	100
30	80
20	60
10	40
0	20
10	0
20	20
30	30
40	40

ABSOLUTE ZERO

Absolute zero is the coldest temperature imaginable. It is -273.15°C (-459.67°F)—much, much colder than anything on Earth. The coldest temperature ever recorded on Earth, at Vostok, Antarctica, was -89°C (-129°F)! In fact, nothing can ever quite reach absolute zero, as all substances always contain a little heat.

freezing point of water (0°C/32°F)

Heat transfer

If you wrap your chilly hands around a mug of hot chocolate, they'll warm up. The flow of heat from warmer things to cooler things is called **heat transfer**. <u>**Heat always flows from warmer substances to cooler ones.**</u>

How does it work? As the tiny molecules in a hot object jiggle around, they bump against the molecules in surrounding objects. This makes them start to move faster, too, and the surrounding objects warm up.

Heat balance

Heat flows from warmer objects to cooler objects next to them, until both objects are the same temperature. They have then reached **thermal equilibrium**. (This means "heat balance.")

Conduction

Conduction is the transfer of heat through a substance or object. For example, if you put a teaspoon in a hot drink, the heat flows up the spoon until the handle feels hot.

TRY THIS

WHAT CONDUCTS HEAT BEST?

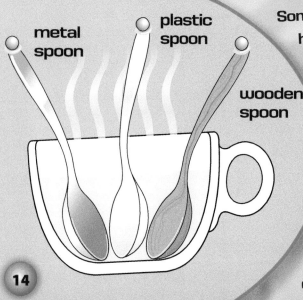

metal spoon

plastic spoon

wooden spoon

Some materials are better at **conducting** heat than others. Test it yourself. Take a wooden spoon, a plastic spoon, and a metal spoon, all of a similar size and shape. Put a dab of cold butter on the end of the handle of each spoon. Stick a frozen pea in the butter. Stand all the spoons in a cup of hot water.

Heat will flow up the spoon handles, melt the butter, and make the pea drop off. Which one falls off first?

Convection

Convection happens when **fluids**, such as water and air, heat up. This makes them expand, or grow, and become less **dense**. Cooler, denser areas of the fluid sink, as they are heavier. Warmer, less dense areas rise to float on top of them. This makes the fluid begin to swirl and mix, spreading heat through the fluid.

This thermal image shows the convection movements of warmer and cooler air above a hot kettle.

Feeling the heat

When you stand in the sunshine, you feel the Sun's heat on your face. But how can this happen? The Sun is 150 million kilometers (93 million miles) away from the Earth, and in between is a **vacuum**, or totally empty space. Heat cannot flow through a vacuum by molecules bumping against each other, as there are no molecules there. So what's going on?

Heat radiation

Heat has another way of spreading out, and it's called **heat radiation**. Hot objects, such as the Sun, a radiator, or a hot iron, give off heat radiation, also called **thermal radiation**. When heat radiation hits another object, it warms it up. Heat radiation is a type of **electromagnetic energy** (a wave of energy that travels across empty space) like light (see page 30).

Outer space is a vacuum, but heat radiation can travel across it. When you stand in sunlight, you absorb the wave and warm up.

When you stand in the sunshine, you feel the Sun's heat radiation on your face. When heat radiation hits an object, it warms it up.

Heat sensors

Some snakes hunt by sensing the heat radiation given off by their prey. They have special organs called heat pits that tell them exactly where the heat is coming from.

Humans cannot do this, but we can detect heat radiation using special infrared cameras. They sense heat and show it as light areas on an image.

This infrared (heat-sensitive) photo shows the heat given off by the snake's prey, a tasty mouse.

Heat pit

A snake's heat-detecting pits are like little cup shapes on the front of its head.

KINETIC AND POTENTIAL ENERGY

Kinetic energy is the energy of movement—the kind of movement you make all day. You climb upstairs or push open a door. A crane lifts pipes up to the top of a building. Planets orbit around the Sun. These are all examples of kinetic energy.

Kinetic energy can also be stored as **potential energy**. Energy held by an object, whether it is kinetic or potential energy, is known as mechanical energy.

As a roller coaster car climbs to the top of a slope, it stores potential energy. This is released as kinetic energy when the roller coaster zooms downhill.

While waiting on a high platform, a bungee jumper holds a store of potential energy. When he jumps off, the energy turns into kinetic energy as he falls.

Energy rush

Gravitational potential energy is stored in an object that is being acted on by gravity. Gravity tries to pull on the object. If other forces hold it still, the potential energy cannot be released. When the object is allowed to move, the potential energy is suddenly released.

Energy in elastic

1. Elastic potential energy can be stored in springs or elastic.

2. You use kinetic energy to stretch an elastic band or squeeze a spring.

3. The kinetic energy you used is stored as potential energy in the object.

4. When you let go, the potential energy is released, and the band or spring moves again as it snaps back into shape.

WATER POWER

This is a hydroelectric dam. It has a vast store of **potential energy**, held in millions of liters of water. When the water is allowed to flow downhill, the potential energy is released as **kinetic energy**. This is very useful, as we can use the kinetic energy to make **electricity**.

1. The dam is a huge, thick wall built across a river valley. As the river flows, water collects behind the dam.

2. Potential energy is stored in the water as it is stopped from flowing any farther.

3. The water is released through pipes at the bottom of the dam.

4. As the water flows through the pipes, it is moving and has kinetic energy.

MOVING NATURE

There is a vast amount of kinetic energy in the natural world around us—in flowing rivers, wind, ocean waves and tides, volcanic eruptions, and earthquakes. We have found ways to capture some of this energy and transform or transfer it into useful forms. Hydroelectric dams are one way. Others include windmills and wind turbines.

Glen Canyon Dam

The dam in the picture is the Glen Canyon Dam on the Colorado River in Arizona. The dam is 216 m (710 feet) high and can hold back 32 cubic km (7.7 cubic miles) of water. It generates around 11 petajoules—or 11,000,000,000,000,000 **joules**—of electricity a year, enough for the needs of more than 600,000 households.

5. In here, the moving water turns wheels called turbines. They are attached to generators—machines that convert kinetic energy into electricity.

CHEMICAL ENERGY

Chemical energy is a form of energy stored in the **chemicals** that make up different substances.

Everything around us is made of **matter** (or stuff). Matter is made of tiny particles called **atoms**. They are usually joined together to make **molecules**. <u>Chemical energy is the energy that holds atoms together in molecules.</u> Each molecule makes a different chemical—a particular type of substance.

a model of an atom

Chemical reactions

A chemical reaction happens when chemicals react with each other and change. Their atoms break apart from each other and make new chemicals. Some chemical reactions turn chemical energy into **heat energy** and give out heat. Some give out light energy, or even **sound energy**—such as an explosion that makes a big BANG!

When a spacecraft takes off, it burns a huge amount of fuel. The chemical energy in the fuel is turned into kinetic energy (movement), heat energy, and sound energy.

Fuel and food

Food is a kind of fuel for our bodies. It contains chemical energy. Our cells turn it into heat and kinetic energy, so that our bodies can keep warm and move around.

Nutrition Facts
Serving Size 1 cup (252g)
Servings Per Container about 2

Amount Per Serving
Calories 270 Calories from Fat 70

	% Daily Value*
Total Fat 7g	11%
Saturated Fat 2.5g	13%
Trans Fat 0g	
Cholesterol 15mg	5%
Sodium 1310mg	54%
Total Carbohydrate 43g	14%
Dietary Fiber 2g	6%
Sugars 9g	
Protein 9g	

Vitamin A 10%	•	Vitamin C 0%
Calcium 2%	•	Iron 10%

* Percent Daily Values are based on a 2,000 calorie diet.

Calorie count

Chemical energy in food is measured in units called **calories** (sometimes written "kcal"). Food packages usually tell you how many calories there are in a given amount, such as 100 g or 1 oz. Find out which foods have the most calories for their weight, by looking at food labels in your kitchen. Write down a selection of foods, find out how many calories they have, and see if you can arrange them in order.

Most foods have information about the energy, or calories, they contain on a label like this.

Food	Calories per 100 g
Sunflower seeds	570
Butter	737
Chocolate cake	380
Carrots	22
Eggs	147
Pasta, uncooked	370

THE ENERGY CYCLE

Chemical energy in food and fuel keeps our world going. But where does it come from? In fact, it doesn't come from our planet at all, but from the Sun.

The Sun is a star—a huge, hot ball of burning gases. It gives out huge amounts of light **energy** that reach Earth. On Earth, plants take in this light energy. They use a process called **photosynthesis** to convert some of it into chemical energy. This is stored in plant matter as the plants grow. <u>**Photosynthesis is the process plants use to convert light energy into chemical energy.**</u>

Passing energy on

Chemical energy in plants can become food or fuel. It is passed on many times as animals eat plants, and other animals eat those animals. This sequence is known as the energy cycle. If it weren't for plants and photosynthesis, we wouldn't be here at all. We depend on plants for food.

Food from the Sun

The energy you use to climb stairs, play sports, or walk to school all comes from the Sun! You get energy from your food, which comes from plants (or animals that eat plants)—and the plants' energy comes from the Sun.

Green and pleasant land

Earth's land looks green from space because of the vast amount of plant matter growing on it.

Food chains

The food chain below is part of the energy cycle.

sun shines on plants and trees

1. Photosynthesis in plants turns light energy from the Sun into chemical energy.

2. Plant matter such as leaves, fruit, and bark is eaten by animals, such as insects and birds.

hawk eats lizard

insect eats plants

lizard eats insect

4. Sometimes, other meat-eaters eat meat-eating animals. Chemical energy is passed along the food chain from one creature to the next.

3. Meat-eating animals eat plant-eating animals. For example, this lizard might eat a leaf-eating insect.

ELECTRICITY

Electricity is one of the most useful of all forms of energy. We use it to power all kinds of everyday appliances, gadgets, vehicles, and machines. Many people depend on electricity every day.

Electricity is a form of energy that comes from **charge**. Charge is a quality of the tiny particles, such as electrons, that make up **atoms**. Charge can make these tiny particles flow through some substances and build up in others.

Static electricity

Static electricity is a buildup of charge in an object. It can escape as a spark, such as a flash of lightning, or the shock you get from a car door.

Lightning is a giant spark of electrical energy leaping between a cloud filled with static electric charge and the ground.

Current electricity

Current electricity is a flow of charged particles through a substance that can **conduct** (carry) them. For example, most metals are good at conducting electricity. That's why we use metal wires to carry a flow of electricity. Plastic does not conduct electricity well. So wires that carry electricity have a plastic covering to keep the electricity safely inside.

ELECTRIC SHOCK!

Our bodies can conduct electricity. If a lot of electrical energy flows through a person, it can be very dangerous. That's why it is important NOT to touch bare electrical wires or stick things into electrical sockets.

WIRED UP

Electricity can be converted into other forms of energy using electrical appliances, such as this string of lights.

1. Electricity flows from a socket along a wire.

3. Electricity flows back to the socket, completing the circuit.

2. As electricity flows through a lamp, the wire inside it heats up and gives out light.

Changing form

When we use electricity in everyday life, we transform electrical energy into other useful forms.

For example, when electricity flows through a narrow wire, the wire gives out heat.

In this way, electricity makes electric heaters, cookers, hair straighteners, and kettles work.

We can also turn electricity into useful kinetic (movement) energy, using a machine called a **motor**.

This train turns a flow of electricity from the wires above the track into movement energy.

Generating electricity

To get the electricity we need, we use other forms of energy, such as the **kinetic energy** of wind or the **chemical energy** in **fuel**. We convert them into electricity using machines called **generators**.

Go with the flow

To make an electrical appliance work, there has to be a flow of electricity right through it and back to the electricity source, such as a **battery**. The electricity doesn't get used up—it keeps flowing around and around the circuit. Instead, fuel or other energy sources get used up to make a constant electricity flow.

If this is confusing, imagine a flowing river turning a waterwheel. The river is like electricity. Its flow provides energy that turns the wheel—but the water itself doesn't get used up.

A battery in this music player releases electrical energy that makes sound energy when the player is switched on.

BATTERY POWER

A battery holds a store of chemical energy. When it is connected to a circuit, the chemical energy is released as electrical energy that flows around the circuit.

LIGHT ENERGY

Light is a form of **energy** made up of high-speed energy waves. Like **heat radiation**, it is a kind of electromagnetic radiation. Light waves are visible, which means that we can sense them with our eyes.

Light waves spread, or **radiate**, out from light sources. The Sun is our main light source. Others include burning flames and electric lights. Like all **electromagnetic energy**, light waves can travel across empty space.

Even moonlight is light from the Sun. The Moon acts as a mirror reflecting sunlight back to Earth. Light from the Sun takes eight minutes to travel to Earth.

LIGHT YEARS

When you look up at the night sky, you can see stars that are many light years away. A light year is the distance that light travels in a year. Light years are used to measure the huge distances in outer space. One light year is about 9.5 million million km (5.9 million million miles)

How waves behave

Light waves travel in straight lines.

They can pass through transparent (see-through) substances but change direction if they bounce, or reflect off objects.

Shadows form when something blocks the flow of light from a light source.

Light bends, or refracts, when it moves from one substance into another—for example, when it passes from glass into air.

beam of light

glass

light refracting

A shadow is the same shape as the object that makes it because light moves in straight lines. Light cannot get past the object, so its shape is recreated as a dark area.

The speed of light

Light waves travel fast—in fact, they go at the fastest possible speed in the universe. **The speed of light and other electromagnetic waves is about 1,000 million kph (621 million mph).**

Seeing

When the Sun shines, or a light is on in a room, light waves bounce off every object and zoom in all directions. Your eyes contain **cells** that can detect when light waves hit them. The cells send signals to your brain, which makes sense of the images it receives.

More electromagnetic waves

Besides light energy, there are several other types of electromagnetic (or EM) wave, with different **wavelengths**. The range of wavelengths is known as the **electromagnetic spectrum** or EMS.

Colors of light

Visible light energy has different colors, each with a slightly different wavelength. As you can see in the diagram below, they are in the same pattern as a rainbow. This is because rainbows happen when sunlight passes through raindrops and splits up into its separate wavelengths. Normal white light is made up of all the colors mixed together.

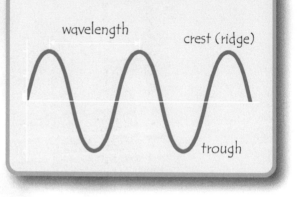

What is wavelength?

A wave's wavelength is the distance from one point on a wave (such as the crest) to the exact same point on the next wave.

wavelength

crest (ridge)

trough

Electromagnetic (EM) waves

Radio waves are very long EM waves. We can modify them (change their shape) and use them to carry signals long distances. They are used in radio and TV broadcasts.

Microwaves are actually quite long EM waves. They can be used to heat up food or carry communications signals.

satellite

cell phone

radio waves

microwaves

longer waves, lower energy

Split light

You can split light into separate colors by shining it through a specially shaped, transparent **prism**. As it enters and leaves the prism, the light refracts, or bends. The longer wavelengths bend more, so the colors spread out and separate.

Electromagnetic spectrum

This diagram shows the range of different wavelengths of electromagnetic energy in the electromagnetic spectrum, from long to short. Shorter waves carry more energy than longer waves.

Infrared radiation is heat radiation. It is also called infrared light. It is used in remote controls.

Ultraviolet radiation is a kind of shortwave light we cannot see. It can give a suntan and damage skin.

X-rays can pass through objects. They are used to make images of our insides.

Gamma rays are the shortest EM waves. They are dangerous because they can kill living things.

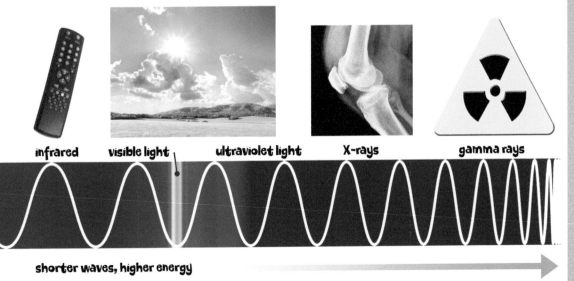

infrared   visible light   ultraviolet light   X-rays   gamma rays

shorter waves, higher energy

Sound Energy

When you hear a sound, you're actually sensing a form of **energy** that travels from a noisy object to your ears. It makes the **molecules** in the air shake and jerk.

Sound energy is given off when an object **vibrates**, or shakes. For example, when you hit a drum, the skin vibrates. When a car engine runs, its parts vibrate. The vibration makes the air molecules around the engine start to vibrate, too. The vibrations spread out like ripples as they pass from one molecule to the next.

When the vibrations reach you, they make parts of your ear vibrate, too. This sends signals to your brain, and you hear the sound.

Some planes can fly faster than the speed of sound, which is about 1,225 kph (761 mph). When this happens, there is a loud bang called a sonic boom as all the sound waves from the plane pile up together. A sonic boom can be powerful enough to smash windows!

Sound waves

Like **electromagnetic energy**, sound travels in waves. However, sound waves do not flow up and down like waves in the sea. **Sound energy is made up of longitudinal waves.**

These waves make particles vibrate forward and back, in the same direction that the wave is traveling in.

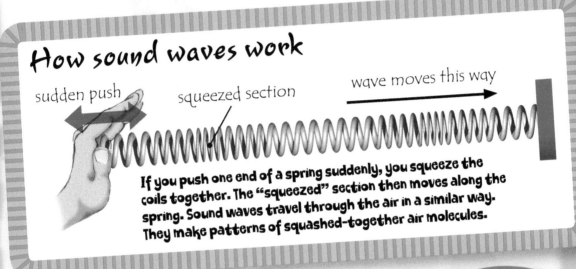

How sound waves work

sudden push

squeezed section

wave moves this way

If you push one end of a spring suddenly, you squeeze the coils together. The "squeezed" section then moves along the spring. Sound waves travel through the air in a similar way. They make patterns of squashed-together air molecules.

Decibels

The volume of a sound depends on how much energy it is carrying. It is measured in units called **decibels** (dB).

Sound	Decibels
Whispering	20dB
Normal talking	40–50dB
Vacuum cleaner	70dB
Rock concert	100dB
Chainsaw	110dB
Jumbo jet takeoff	140dB
Blue whale song	190dB

TRY THIS

Feel sound waves

You can feel sound waves through an empty plastic bottle, as they will make it vibrate. Hold the bottle up against a radio or stereo speaker with music playing. You should be able to feel the vibrations in your hand.

NUCLEAR ENERGY

Nuclear energy is a form of **energy** held inside **atoms**—the tiny units that make up **matter**. This form of energy holds atoms together. When atoms split apart, the energy is released.

Nuclear energy gets its name from the central part, or **nucleus**, of an atom. This form of energy is also called **nuclear radiation**, as it spreads, or **radiates**, out from an atom's nucleus.

Radioactivity

Some substances are naturally **radioactive**. This means their nuclei give out nuclear radiation. Sometimes this is in the form of tiny particles. Sometimes it's in the form of gamma rays, a kind of **electromagnetic energy**.

Radioactive substances include radium, uranium, and polonium. They are also dangerous. Nuclear radiation can be harmful and make us ill.

Unfortunately, nuclear energy can be used in a destructive way. This mushroom cloud is from a huge, powerful atom bomb.

Nuclear reactions

Nuclear radiation can be useful, too. We can use it to make **electricity**. In nuclear power stations, we control radiation carefully to create a nuclear chain reaction. This gives out heat, which we use to power **generators** that make electricity. The diagram below shows how it works.

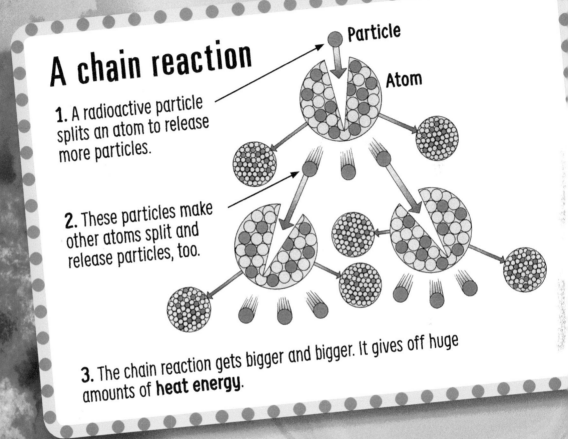

A chain reaction

Particle

Atom

1. A radioactive particle splits an atom to release more particles.

2. These particles make other atoms split and release particles, too.

3. The chain reaction gets bigger and bigger. It gives off huge amounts of **heat energy**.

Other uses of nuclear energy

Nuclear energy has other uses, too. For example, a beam of nuclear radiation is used to kill germs on surgical tools and bandages before they are used. X-ray photography works by passing a small amount of radiation through the body and detecting how it comes back out.

ENERGY SUPPLIES

We use up a lot of **energy**. Modern homes are full of electric lights, appliances, radiators, stoves, and boilers that all need energy to run. We also use energy for making and transporting goods, and for traveling in cars, buses, trains, and planes.

We get the energy we need from many sources. The chart on the right shows some of the main ones, where they are from, and what form of energy they are. Some energy sources are used directly—for example oil can be burned to heat homes. Most can also be converted into **electricity**.

Energy source	Form of energy	From
Oil	Chemical	Underground
Coal	Chemical	Underground
Wood	Chemical	Plants
Natural gas	Chemical	Underground
Wind	Kinetic	Air
Waves	Kinetic	Sea
Flowing water	Kinetic	Rivers
Tidal energy	Kinetic	Sea
Solar energy	Light	Sun
Geothermal	Heat	Underground
Nuclear	Nuclear	Atoms

Fossil fuels

Oil, coal, and natural gas are known as **fossil fuels**. They formed in prehistoric times from plant and animal **matter**. We now extract them from underground. We are using up fossil fuels far faster than they can form, so they will eventually run out.

Renewables

Renewable energy sources do not get used up. However much we use them, they will keep providing more energy. They include wind, waves, and tides. Using these energy sources can be difficult and expensive. So scientists are working on new and better ways to collect renewable energy. We will need renewable energy sources to replace fossil fuels as they run out.

Wind turbines like these use kinetic energy from the wind to turn their blades. A generator then converts the turning movement into an electricity supply.

A geothermal plant uses the heat deep inside Earth to heat water and make steam. The steam turns turbines and generates a supply of electricity.

ENERGY MAP

Energy is everywhere! This map shows how energy from different sources can be transformed and transferred many times and in many different ways as we use it.

Oil

Oil from underground is chemical energy.

Gas

Gas from underground is chemical energy.

Power plant

Coal and gas power plants turn chemical energy into heat energy, heat energy into kinetic energy, and kinetic energy into electricity.

Coal

Coal from underground is chemical energy.

City or town

Wind farm

A wind farm uses kinetic energy. Wind turbines turn kinetic energy into electricity.

Hydroelectric dam

A hydroelectric dam uses kinetic energy. Hydroelectric dams turn kinetic energy into electricity.

Solar power plant

Solar power is light energy. Solar panels turn light energy into electricity.

Nuclear power plant

A nuclear power plant uses nuclear energy. Nuclear power plants turn nuclear energy into heat energy, heat energy into kinetic energy, and kinetic energy into electricity.

Vehicle engines turn chemical energy in oil into heat and movement.

A stereo system turns electricity into sound and heat energy.

City traffic lights and streetlights turn electricity into light energy.

Lightbulbs turn electricity into light and heat energy.

A TV turns electricity into light, sound, and heat energy.

Fires, stoves, boilers, and oil heaters turn chemical energy in oil, coal, and gas into heat energy.

Electricity is transferred along cables to homes and other places where it is needed.

An iron turns electricity into heat energy.

Electric buses and wheelchairs turn electricity into kinetic energy.

A fan turns electricity into kinetic energy and sound energy.

A laptop turns electricity into light, sound, and heat energy.

Timeline

These are some key dates and events in the history of the science of energy.

c. 600 BCE — Ancient Greek thinker Thales of Miletus studies static electric sparks.

c. 1000 CE — Arabic scientist Alhazen studies the way light travels and refracts (bends).

1593 — Galileo Galilei and other scientists invent the first thermometers.

1704 — Isaac Newton describes the behavior of light and **prisms**.

1752 — American scientist Benjamin Franklin shows that lightning is a form of **electricity** and uses it to make an electric current flow along a wet string.

1799 — Alessandro Volta of Italy makes the Voltaic pile, the first electric **battery**.

1820 — Danish scientist Hans Ørsted discovers that wire with electricity running through it becomes magnetic—one of the first pieces of evidence for **electromagnetic energy**.

1821 — British scientist and inventor Michael Faraday invents the **motor**, which transforms electricity into kinetic (movement) energy.

1831 — Michael Faraday invents the **generator**, which transforms kinetic (movement) energy into electricity.

1845 — British scientist James Prescott Joule does experiments that show how energy can be transformed from one form to another.

1860s — British scientist James Clerk Maxwell studies electromagnetism and shows how light is a form of electromagnetic energy.

1888 — German scientist Heinrich Hertz demonstrates the existence of radio waves, a form of electromagnetic energy.

1895 — Italian inventor Guglielmo Marconi develops a way of using radio waves to carry messages.

1896 — French scientist Henri Becquerel discovers a new form of energy, **radioactivity**.

1896–99 — Becquerel's colleagues Pierre and Marie Curie study radioactivity and find out how it works.

1905 — German scientist Albert Einstein publishes his ideas on light, mass, and energy, including his equation $E=mc^2$ (which means that **matter** is a form of energy).

1911 — New Zealand-born British scientist Ernest Rutherford does experiments that reveal that an **atom** has a **nucleus** in the middle.

WHO'S WHO?

These famous scientists made great discoveries about energy and its various forms.

Marie Curie (1867–1934) and Pierre Curie (1859-1906)
Marie Curie was born in Poland. She moved to Paris and worked with her French husband, Pierre Curie, on radioactivity (**nuclear energy**). They discovered how it worked, where it came from, and gave it its name.

Thomas Edison (1847–1931)
Edison was a great American scientist and inventor. Among other things, he invented a kind of lightbulb and the phonograph, a way of recording sound.

Albert Einstein (1879–1955)
This famous German scientist came up with many very important theories about light and other forms of electromagnetic energy. He saw how energy and matter are in fact the same thing and can be converted into each other.

Michael Faraday (1791–1867)
British scientist Faraday found out a lot about the relationship between electricity and magnetism. He used his discoveries to invent the motor and the generator, which convert electricity into movement and vice versa. They are still essential today, for creating electricity supplies and making electrical appliances work.

Benjamin Franklin (1706–1790)
This American scientist did an experiment with lightning, gathering an electric current from it. He also invented the lightning conductor, a structure that carries electricity safely to the ground in a thunderstorm.

James Prescott Joule (1818–1889)
British scientist Joule experimented with electricity, **kinetic energy**, and **heat energy** to show how forms of energy can change into each other. He also showed that energy cannot be created or destroyed—the basis of the **Law of Conservation of Energy**.

James Clerk Maxwell (1831–1879)
This British scientist studied electromagnetic energy. He discovered how it worked and that it could take various forms.

Isaac Newton (1642–1727)
British-born Newton was one of the greatest scientists ever. He studied how objects move, how gravity works, and how light travels, refracts, and splits into colors. He developed the laws of motion, which explain what happens when kinetic energy makes things move.

Nikola Tesla (1856–1943)
This important Croatian scientist and engineer studied and contributed to many fields of energy science. This included electromagnetism (especially radio waves), electricity, and nuclear energy.

Energy Quiz

Test your memory and research skills with this quiz. All the answers to these questions can be found in the pages of this book.

1. What is the definition of **energy**?

2. When energy **dissipates**, it usually ends up as which energy form?

3. What kind of wave is a sound wave?

4. When objects rub together as they move, **kinetic energy** is turned into **heat energy**. What is the rubbing called?

5. What units are used to measure the amount of **chemical energy** in food?

6. What is stored energy called?

7. Name three types of **electromagnetic energy** besides visible light.

8. Where does solar energy come from?

9. Which part of an **atom** does **nuclear energy** come from?

10. What is the name of a device that turns kinetic energy into **electricity**?

11. What is a light year?

12. What units are sound volume measured in?

Answers on page 47

Glossary

absolute zero coldest imaginable temperature in which a substance contains no heat at all

atoms tiny units that all matter is made from

battery store of potential electrical energy held in chemical form

calorie (kcal) unit used to measure the amount of chemical energy in food

cells tiny units that make up the bodies of humans and other living things

charge quality of some of the tiny particles that make up atoms. Charge can be positive (+) or negative (-).

chemical particular substance, made up of one type of molecule

chemical energy form of energy that holds atoms together to form molecules. Chemical energy is stored in substances.

conduct to carry a form of energy such as heat or electricity. For example, copper wire can conduct electricity.

convection way heat energy spreads through fluids by making them swirl and mix

current electricity electricity that flows through a substance, for example along a wire

decibel (dB) unit used to measure the volume or loudness of sound energy

dense closely compacted in substance

dissipate when energy dissipates, it escapes from an object or energy transformation, usually becoming heat energy

efficient efficient machines and systems use or transform energy without allowing very much of it to dissipate or escape

electricity form of energy caused by a buildup or flow of charged particles

electromagnetic energy form of energy made up of waves. There are several kinds of electromagnetic energy, including light, X-rays, and radio waves.

electromagnetic spectrum range of different types of electromagnetic energy, arranged according to their wavelengths

energy ability to do work

energy conversion change from one form of energy into another

energy-efficient see efficient

energy transfer movement of energy from one place to another, even when it does not change form

energy transformation change from one form of energy into another

fluid liquid or gas

fossil fuel fuels such as oil and coal that are made from fossilized remains of living things

friction force that converts kinetic energy into heat when moving objects rub or drag against each other

fuel substance that contains chemical energy and that is burned to release kinetic energy or heat energy

generator device that converts kinetic energy into electricity

heat energy form of energy caused by the movement of atoms and molecules in a substance

heat radiation form of electromagnetic energy given off by hot objects

heat transfer spread of heat from a warm object to a cooler one

joule unit used to measure energy

kinetic energy energy in moving objects

Law of Conservation of Energy law that states that energy cannot be created or destroyed but can only change from one form to another

matter stuff, substances or materials that are real and take up space

molecule unit of a chemical, made up of one or more atoms

motor device that turns electrical energy into kinetic energy

nuclear energy energy held in or given off by the nucleus of an atom

nuclear radiation nuclear energy that is given out by the atoms of some substances

nucleus central part of an atom

photosynthesis process plants use to convert light energy in sunlight into chemical energy in their cells

potential energy stored energy

prism piece of glass, often triangle-shaped, that splits light up into its colors

radiate to spread out from a source

radioactivity release of nuclear energy from the atoms of some substances

renewable energy energy sources such as wind, that can be replaced by natural forces when we use them

sound energy form of energy that makes a wave of moving particles spread though a medium such as air

static electricity build up of charged particles that can result in a spark

thermal to do with heat

thermal equilibrium balance that happens when heat energy has spread from one object into another until they are the same temperature

thermal radiation see heat radiation

thermometer device for measuring temperature

turbine device that turns a flow of kinetic energy, such as wind, into a rotating movement

vacuum empty space

vibrate to shake back and forth

wavelength measurement from one point on a wave (such as its highest point) to the same point on the next wave

Find Out More

Books

Ballard, Carol; Dreier, David L.; Morgan, Sally; and Smuskiewicz, Alfred J., *Energy (Physical Science in Depth series)*. Chicago: Heinemann Library, 2008.

Gifford, Clive, *Energy (Planet Under Pressure series)*. Chicago: Heinemann Library, 2006.

Landau, Elaine, *The History of Energy*. New York: Lerner, 2008.

Oxlade, Chris, and Jennings, Terry J., *Energy (Science Alive series)*. Mankato, MN: Smart Apple Media, 2009.

Silverman, Buffy, *Saving Energy (Do It Yourself series)*. Chicago: Heinemann Library, 2008.

Woodford, Chris, *Energy (See for Yourself series)*. New York: DK Publishers, 2007.

Websites

http://www.energyquest.ca.gov/
Energy Quest
Fun site all about energy, with useful facts, interactive activities, puzzles, and games.

http://www.eia.doe.gov/kids/
Energy Kids' Page
All-round introduction to energy with facts, quizzes, games, and classroom activities.

http://clarkenergy.apogee.net/kids/fe_ifrm.aspx
Clark Energy Kids' Corner
Information on energy, including a series of energy experiments to try.

Answers to quiz on page 44

1. Energy is the ability to do work.
2. Heat energy.
3. Longitudinal wave.
4. Friction.
5. Calories.
6. Potential energy.
7. Any of: gamma rays, X-rays, microwaves, radio waves, ultraviolet radiation, and infrared (or heat) radiation.
8. The Sun.
9. The nucleus.
10. A generator.
11. The distance light travels in a year.
12. Decibels.

Index